Philip Steele

The Tactics of Terror

Macdonald

A MACDONALD BOOK

© Philip Steele, 1986

First published in Great Britain in 1986 by
Macdonald & Co. (Publishers) Ltd
London and Sydney
A BPCC plc company

ISBN 0 356 11617 4

Editor Donna Bailey
Production Rosemary Bishop
Picture Research Elizabeth Loving

Printed in Great Britain by
Purnell Book Production Ltd
Member of the BPCC Group

Macdonald & Co. (Publishers) Ltd
Greater London House
Hampstead Road
London NW1 7QX

BRITISH LIBRARY
CATALOGUING IN PUBLICATION DATA

Steele, Philip
   The tactics of terror. – (Debates)
   1.Terrorism
   I.Title   II. Series
   322.4'2   HV 6431
   ISBN 0-356-11617-4

Contents

A timetable

Terrorism has long been one of the world's most pressing problems, and one which seems to defy solutions. The following news items were recorded in the British press in 1985. They are remarkable events which today seem only too routine:

Saturday 22 June A car is surrounded in Glasgow, Scotland. Police detectives sieze three men and two women under the Prevention of Terrorism Act. Is this an active service unit of the IRA? Police find a list of twelve English seaside resorts and the name of a London hotel. Has another bombing campaign been thwarted?

Sunday 23 June London's Buckingham Palace Road: the Rubens Hotel is searched. In Room 112 the police find a 2.25 kg bomb with a long-delay fuse. It could explode if tampered with, but it is defused by experts.

Monday 24 June Coastal towns placed on special alert. Great Yarmouth searched.

Tuesday 25 June Further arrests in Scotland and England. Sir Kenneth Newman, of London's Metropolitan Police, placed in charge of operations.

Wednesday 26 June Torquay searched. Police computers run checks.

Thursday 27 June Further arrests. Suspects detained.

Friday 28 June Glasgow: hoard of weapons and bomb-making equipment uncovered.

Saturday 29 June Patrick Joseph Magee of Belfast charged with the murder of five people at Brighton's Grand Hotel on 12 October 1984, at the start of the hotel bombing campaign. The victims were members of the Conservative Party, gathering for their annual conference. Magee faced trial in May 1986; found guilty of murder of five people, victims of the IRA bomb.

A secret war? In 1985 headlines such as these in the British press were concerned with bomb plots, murder, kidnapping and

for terror

arson. Armoured cars patrolled the streets of Belfast. The United Kingdom may not have been at war, but was it at peace?

Behind the news stories lay evidence of another kind of war. Terrorists had been trained to use weapons and explosives, to resist interrogation, to act with military precision. Security forces had learned to use the most modern weapons and communications systems, to fight on home territory and set up networks of informers.

The aim of the Provisional IRA was the withdrawal of British troops from Northern Ireland, and the establishment of a united Republic. Was their cause just or unjust? Were their methods moral or immoral? How could the bombing of English hotels further their aim? Was the British government responsible for the problem or was the Irish government? Was it all a question of history, or religion, or politics?

The need for debate Faced with such a tangle of problems, the public remained and remains bemused. Is there any difference between terrorists and freedom fighters or guerrillas? Can states be terrorist too? What *is* terrorism? The popular press often

reports acts of terror in a sensationalist way, and fails to consider the real issues at stake.

It is true that the questions, moral and practical, are not always easy to answer. They must however be raised, or there is no hope of a peaceful solution: ignorance breeds violence. This book aims to raise some of those questions, and outline the arena of debate.

Britain at peace? An army patrol on Belfast's Falls Road check their riot gear before charging a Republican demonstration.

Opposite October 1984: Brighton, England. A great gash in the facade of the Grand Hotel reveals where a Provisional IRA bomb killed five people.

> 'We declare the right of the people of Ireland to the ownership of Ireland . . . to be sovereign . . .' *1916 proclamation on behalf of the Provisional Government of Ireland*

> 'Last week the police announced they had discovered an IRA plan to plant bombs in 12 seaside resorts. They . . . appeared to have destroyed one of the Provisional IRA's active service units'. The Sunday Times, *30 June 1985*

A worldwide

O n Easter Sunday 1986 a British soldier in Northern Ireland was shot in the face by a Republican sniper. On the same day Pope John Paul II, preaching in St Peter's Square, Rome, identified terrorism as one of the most urgent problems facing the international community.

During the period 1970–85 it is estimated that 40,394 people were killed by terrorists throughout the world, in 22,171 separate incidents. Violence spread to almost every corner of the globe, and in 1985 even hitherto peaceful countries such as Nepal and Norway witnessed acts of terror.

Just another year? A selective diary for just the first six months of 1985 reveals the extent to which terrorism dominated international headlines:

January 2, *USA* Prisoners hijack plane to Cuba. ***28,*** *Portugal* Terrorists fire mortar bombs at NATO ships.

February 1, *West Germany* Industrialist dies after being shot by Red Army Faction (RAF). ***4,*** *UK* Kashmiri students jailed for murder of Indian diplomat. ***7,*** *Poland* Two secret policemen jailed for murder of pro-Solidarity priest. ***10,*** *Lebanon* Israeli planes bomb Palestinian base. Car bomb kills two. ***12,*** *UK* Israeli businessman jailed for kidnap of former Nigerian politician. ***20,*** *UK* Libyan students jailed for 1984 bombing campaign. ***23,*** *Lebanon* Airport guard hijacks jet. *France* Bomb kills 17 at Paris branch of Marks & Spencer. ***27,*** *Austria* Plane forced down at Vienna by two Syrians deported from West Germany. ***28,*** *Northern Ireland* Provisional IRA mortar police station, nine killed.

March 4, *Lebanon* Mosque bomb kills 15. ***7,*** *UK* Two jailed for bombings by Provisional IRA. ***8,*** *Lebanon* Car bomb kills 62. ***10,*** *Lebanon* Twelve Israeli troops killed by suicide attack. ***17,*** *Saudi Arabia* Plane seized but hijacker killed. ***21,*** *South Africa* Police shoot 19 Blacks at funeral. Police later blamed by judicial inquiry. ***28,*** *Irish Republic* Three sentenced to death for killing policeman during Provisional IRA bank raid.

April 2, *West Germany* Leftist terrorists Brigitte Mohnhaupt and Christian Klar jailed for murder. ***26,*** *Nigeria* Hundreds reported killed in religious terror.

May 12, *India* Death toll in bombing reaches 87. ***14,*** *Sri Lanka* Tamils gun down 86 in

Below September 1985: Larnaca, Cyprus. Three were killed in this attack by a Palestinian terrorist group, which included a British supporter. The PLO disassociated themselves from the incident.

'. . . the international community must step up to this problem and deal with it unequivocally.'
George P. Shultz, US Secretary of State

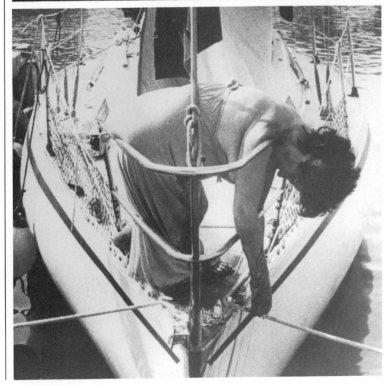

problem?

street. *Afghanistan* Soviet troops reported to have killed some 1,000 civilians. *20, Northern Ireland* Provisional IRA bomb attack kills four police.

June 6, USA Senate agrees aid for Contras in Nicaragua. *11, Lebanon* Shiite gunmen hijack Jordanian jet. Refused a landing at Tunis, they return to Beirut, release passengers and blow up plane. *14, Northern Ireland* Six Ulster Volunteer Force (UVF) terrorists jailed for sectarian murders. *Greece* TWA airliner hijacked on flight from Athens, taken to Beirut, Algiers and back to Beirut. One US citizen killed and 39 hostages subsequently held at secret Beirut location. *19, West Germany* Bomb kills three at Frankfurt Airport. *22, Norway* Plane hijacked between Trondheim and Oslo.

23, Japan Bomb explodes when baggage from Canadian Pacific plane unloaded. *UK* Provisional IRA Bomb defused at London hotel. *29, UK* Belfast man charged with murder following October bombing of hotel by Provisional IRA.

A Third World War? This bewildering array of incidents poses many questions. Were any attacks connected, or even coordinated? Were any justified, or none? Could they have been prevented? Was there a pattern? Could it be that the Third World War had already arrived, but that it was unacknowledged: not set warfare with standing armies, but thousands of brutal backstreet confrontations between nation states and their opponents?

November 1985: an EgyptAir jet at Malta's Luqa Airport, after being hijacked on a flight from Athens to Cairo. Sixty people died during a rescue bid by Egyptian commandos.

'The hijacking of TWA Flight 847 . . . registered on the world's terrorist monitoring computers as the twentieth hijack of 1985.'

New Society, 28 June 1985

Is terrorism

> ## 'All the bourgeois shall be blown up!'
> *French anarchist song, 1890s*

Is terrorism an invention of the twentieth century? In the press, our own troubled times are often contrasted with the 'good old days' when the rule of law was accepted unchallenged. It is true that modern communications and weapons may have changed the *nature* of the problem, but is the problem itself a new one?

Murderers and martyrs Could it be that the modern decline in religious beliefs might account for the growing violence in our society? It is true that in the past many faiths have exercised a moderating and civilizing influence. However, adherents of those same faiths have also used terror against their opponents throughout history.

During the Middle Ages it was an Ismaili Moslem sect based in Persia and Syria that terrorized the contemporary world. Its chief, known as Sheikh al Jebel ('Old Man of the Mountains') ordered the murder of prominent people. The devoted killers became known as *hāshshāshin* ('takers of the drug hashish') and it is from this term that our word 'assassin' is derived. Christians too regularly used tactics of terror. They massacred and tortured other Christians whom they held to be 'heretics'. The Spanish Inquisition, founded in 1478, tortured and burned Christians, converted Moslems and Jews, as well as political enemies of the Popes and the Spanish monarchy.

For the greater good? Are contemporary political theories to blame for the rise in terrorism? Is the blurred distinction between crime and political action a symptom of our age? Throughout history, European and Asian bandits waylaid rich travellers and robbed and murdered. Many professed political motives. Marco Scierra, a brigand in sixteenth century Naples, said that he was 'sent by God against usurers and possessors of unproductive wealth'. The legendary outlaw Robin Hood has long been a popular hero. To the Sheriff of Nottingham, would he have been a terrorist?

Institutionalized terror in history: the execution of Louis XVI in 1793. The French revolutionaries toppled a corrupt monarchy, but then declared a new 'Reign of Terror'.

something new?

What of state terror? Again, it would seem that it has a long history. Many Roman emperors ruled through terror, and the *pax romana*, the peace of the Roman empire, was only made possible by acts of ruthless atrocity. The dungeon and torture chamber are well known as symbols of medieval society, as is the guillotine of the French Revolution, when the new rulers sought to cow their opponents with a 'Reign of Terror'.

Already by the nineteenth century terrorism had taken on its modern appearance. The repressive rulers of Tsarist Russia were shaken by a series of assassinations and random acts of violence. Anarchists created havoc throughout Europe and America, placing bombs in public places and killing heads of state: President Sadi Carnot of France in 1894, King Umberto of Italy in 1900, President McKinley of the USA in 1901. But this was no new phenomenon: acts of terror stretch into the distant past,

> '*Between the reign of Elizabeth and that of William and Mary there were thirty or forty English plots to assassinate the sovereign.*'
>
> David Rapoport *in* Assassination and Terrorism, *1971*

far beyond the assassination of Julius Caesar in 44BC.

Lessons of history Why does terrorism reappear over the ages? Is it because people are forever struggling against repressive forces to bring in new ideas? Could it be that history is a series of inevitable confrontations between old and new ideas, in which the innocent suffer the most and violence is the price of change? Many contemporary crises have their roots in past centuries. The lessons of history cannot be ignored if these problems are to be solved.

The funeral of hunger striker Bobby Sands. Northern Ireland is one of today's worst trouble spots, but the origins of the crisis stretch back over centuries.

What is meant by terrorism?

Journalists and politicians use the term 'terrorism' very freely. Debate demands that we should seek a more precise definition. Under most legal systems, no distinction is made between the terrorist and the common criminal: judges tend to dismiss a political motivation as irrelevant in court. Is there then no difference between a killing by the Mafia or some other criminal gang, and the murder of, say, a policeman by a Basque separatist? According to most judges, there is not.

Terrorists would disagree. They believe that their political cause transcends any obligation to the legal code, and very often refuse to recognize the legitimacy of the court that tries them. The Russian anarchist Piotr Kropotkin (1842–1921), a relatively moderate revolutionary, dismissed legality in no uncertain terms. He called for 'permanent revolt by word of mouth, in writing, by the dagger, the rifle, dynamite . . . Everything is good for us which falls outside legality . . .'.

By what terms therefore can we judge terrorists? If they are not common criminals, are their acts to be pardoned in the light of some natural justice for which they are struggling? Does the validity of the cause determine whether the act of terror is justified, or the methods employed?

The 'terrorist' will sometimes refer to him or herself by this term, but more often prefers to use words such as 'guerrilla' or 'freedom fighter'. The word 'guerrilla' means someone who fights a war by irregular methods. The term often implies that the person in question is part of a group organized on military lines, which fights or harries regular troops but avoids pitched battle. The term 'freedom fighter' suggests that the person is fighting an oppressive government or colonial power.

Definitions 'Terrorism' therefore means different things to different people. Perhaps for a definition we should turn to the root of the word itself. It suggests that terrorists aim to create a climate of *fear* in society. So of course do members of the Mafia. In normal usage, however, terrorism also implies additional *political* motivation. Terror is induced so that society may be transformed in some way.

What constitutes an act of terror? Again, there are many possible viewpoints. To most people, armed violence which en-

Olof Palme addressing crowds during the run-up to the Swedish general election in the autumn of 1985. He was soon to be assassinated by a right-wing extremist. Terrorism is preventing politicians freely associating with their constituents.

terrorism . . . *n. 1 the use of terrorizing methods 2 the state of fear and submission so produced 3 a method of resisting a government or of governing by deliberate acts of violence.* Hamlyn Encyclopedic World Dictionary

dangers human life would be an act of terror. But does the victim have to be innocent? Is the murder of a tyrant also a terrorist act? Depriving someone of their liberty, or kidnapping, is also commonly deemed to be terrorism, as are bank raids, acts of sabotage and arson, although they do not necessarily endanger human life. Does society's definition of terrorism sometimes depend on the value it places on property as much as on human life?

The term 'terrorist' is usually used to describe opponents of an established government or regime. Could it be that this convention is encouraged by the fact that in most countries the media and judiciary are inextricably connected with the machinery of state? Many states are themselves terrorist, using acts of violence to intimidate their opponents.

Such diverse views of terrorism cannot easily be reconciled within a single definition: the term is normally used subjectively. A working definition, however, might be as follows: terrorism is an act of violence carried out by individual, group or state, which aims to create fear and so precipitate social change or promote political or religious beliefs.

The aftermath of a car bomb placed outside Harrods in London in 1983. The Provisional IRA were responsible. What cause can justify the murder of innocent passers-by?

'. . . Now we have our backs to the wall . . . we begin to speak the only language they understand – violence.' Free Wales Army statement

Terror on

In 1968 Paris was shaken by a series of mass demonstrations. The demonstrations turned into riots. Students occupied their universities and workers took over their factories. It looked as though the government itself would fall. Could this be regarded as terrorism in action? The demonstrations were not armed, but were violent, and had social change as their motivation. According to the demonstrators, however, the only terror was induced by the brutal reaction of the French riot police to legitimate demonstrations. They felt that it was the state's tactics which were terrorist.

In the 1980s England also saw a series of urban riots, in Brixton, London; Toxteth, Liverpool; St Paul's, Bristol, and many other centres. This time there was no overt political motive. Arson, looting and fighting with the police seemed to erupt spontaneously. Was this the result of criminality? Or was it the result of frustration at unemployment, poverty, racist attitudes and officious policing? And was it terrorist? Little evidence was produced to show that the riots were organized in advance, although terror was clearly the immediate aim of the rioters.

Right Riot police in action, Paris 1968. The police stand at the front line between the state and its citizens. Who is terrorizing whom?

widespread urban terror, even if they were sparked off by and countered with the terror of the ruling classes towards them. It was the violence of the urban rabble, the *sans-culottes*, which made possible the French Revolution of 1789. In the sprawling, impersonal cities of the twentieth century, the pressures of everyday life are such that armed violence would seem to be inevitable. Terrorism grows in the slum and shanty town; many city-based terrorist groups, 'urban guerrillas' such as the Uruguayan

> '*Good policing will be of no avail unless we also tackle and eliminate basic flaws in our society.*'
>
> Lord Justice Scarman, 1981

From riot to terror? Is there a danger that a demonstration can turn into spontaneous rioting, and rioting to organized terror? The *jacqueries* and peasants' revolts of medieval Europe certainly unleashed

the streets ?

Tupamaros, became active in the 1960s and 70s, engaging in kidnapping, bank raids and murder.

Is there any connection between demonstrating, rioting and terrorist activities? Or is each simply a different way of reacting to the same oppression? In an urban riot the looter may be seen as a terrorist, a criminal, or as a poor man retrieving what should be his by right. To what extent does personal gain play a part in terrorist motivation?

It often serves the interest of an oppressive state to bracket all forms of opposition together with terrorism. Demonstrations, even peaceful ones, are declared illegal, so that they can be termed 'criminal'. Police agents may mingle with the crowd and spur people on to acts of violence, so that their cause becomes discredited. Less subtle policing aims to terrorize the demonstrators by the use of live ammunition, plastic bullets, truncheons, tear-gas, water cannon, dogs, horses, random arrests and detention. Are such methods necessary to maintain law and order?

Mob rule? The English monk Alcuin (735–804), adviser to the great Charlemagne, wrote: 'Nor should we listen to those who say, "The voice of the people is the voice of God", for the turbulence of the mob is always close to insanity.' *Is* there something about crowd behaviour which encourages the individual to act violently? Are leaders

'The only genuine, long-range solution for what has happened lies in an attack . . . upon the conditions that breed despair and violence . . . ignorance, discrimination, slums, poverty, disease, not enough jobs.'

President Lyndon B. Johnson, 1968

who make use of the volatile nature of the crowd in order to organize riots or terror campaigns manipulating, or mobilizing and helping to articulate grievances? Does the answer depend on the justice of their cause?

Freedom fighters? or murderers?

In 1952 Jomo Kenyatta, leader of the Kenyan struggle for independence, was sentenced to hard labour by the British authorities. However, by the time of his death in 1979, the man the press had branded a 'terrorist' was being hailed by the British as the 'grand old man' of African politics. Do historical perspectives change our attitudes?

Value judgements? Language is often used subjectively or emotionally, and the use of the word 'terrorist' may depend upon the political viewpoint of the speaker. For example, a Soviet politician might consider the Afghani Mujihadeen as terrorists, whilst an American might see them as freedom fighters. Both Soviet and American might refer to Shiite Moslems in Lebanon as terrorists however, and Soviet and American accusations might be entirely reversed when considering the Nicaraguan Contras.

What other considerations can decide whether we see someone as a 'terrorist' or as 'freedom fighter'? Religion? Class or social background? One's generation? Education and upbringing? Nationality?

What differentiates the heroes and villians? During the Second World War many French people offered fierce resistance to the Nazi troops of occupation. Their bravery made them the heroes of post-war Europe, and although their actions had been violent and illegal, nobody considered them to be terrorists. Can it therefore be said that many of us draw a distinction between good laws and bad laws, and justify tactics of terror *under certain circumstances*?

War by any other name? Consider the behaviour of soldiers during a war. Marines are trained to murder by stealth, airmen to drop bombs on innocent civilians, and killers are welcomed home as heroes. In what way does their behaviour differ from that of terrorists? In a legal declaration of war? Wars are rarely voted for in a referendum, and very often are never formally declared. International agreements such as the Geneva Convention may regulate warfare and relieve its suffering, but they do not mitigate its violence or aggression.

Many terrorists and freedom fighters argue that whereas powerful states can remedy an injustice by acts of war, or by political or economic action, a group that is unable to command such power, as a result of poverty, oppression or dispossession, has little choice but to resort to acts of terror. Are their acts then no more blameworthy than those of major powers engaged in formal warfare?

Opponents of terrorism might argue that 'two wrongs do not make a right'; that civilization depends upon a rigid interpretation of law and order. The issues are important ones, and do not deserve to become confused with mere propaganda. Ultimately, it is up to the individual to decide where he or she will draw the line between what is considered moral or immoral.

> 'History is the property of the winners.'
> Noam Chomsky, 1979

Left The freedom fighter: a Frelimo guerrilla during the 1964-74 struggle to liberate Mozambique from colonial rule by the Portuguese. To the colonists he would be considered a 'terrorist'.

> 'The British who arm their commandos with knives and instruct them to kill . . . from the rear – protested most vigorously when such tactics were applied to themselves.'
> George Grivas, leader of EOKA, in Memoirs, 1964

For the good of the cause?

In October 1980, 79 travellers were killed by right-wing terrorists at the railway station in Bologna, Italy. At that time there were some 125 organizations in the world which advocated or practised terrorist methods. A great many of them were groups whose aim was to change the structure of society. They followed theories of politics, or ideologies, which preferred revolution to reform. How do professed idealists justify acts of violence? Do they see terror as a means to an end, or do they advocate a terrorist state?

A new social order? Some terrorist groups are made up of anarchists. They believe that society should be run through the co-operation of individuals and groupings such as trade unions, rather than by rule of government. Many anarchists, therefore, believe in the essential goodness of the individual, and reject the use of terror. Others, however, argue that assassination and bombing are the only way to demoralize an apparently omnipotent, terrorist state.

The 1977 funeral of West German revolutionaries Andreas Baader and Gudrun Ensslin. The Baader-Meinhof group used terrorist tactics to further their cause.

The Red Brigades on trial in Turin, Italy. The defendants are led to the police van in chains.

Many terrorists commit their acts in the name of socialism or communism, but the majority of socialists and communists reject terrorist tactics as such. Karl Marx (1818–83) saw communism as the end product of an inevitable economic process. The new era was to be introduced less by acts of individual terror than by a mass revolution of the working classes. It was argued that there was no need to provoke an uprising by acts of violence; the injustices were there for all to see, and the revolution was a matter of course. In reality, was it unrealistic to expect such revolutions to occur without acts of terror? Does the breakdown of any established order result in terror? Can a terrorist state be forced from power by non-terrorist methods? The October Revolution of 1917 was preceded and followed by campaigns of terror by both sides.

What of the profit-based economic order that the anarchists and communists wish to overthrow? Do capitalists also resort to terrorism? In some socialist states, where they form a counter-revolutionary minority, they have done so. They have also used state terrorism. In general, however, capitalist states have found that the best way to combat contrary political movements and maintain power is to permit a degree of liberal reform.

Such solutions are totally rejected by fascists and neofascists. Their ideal social order is one subjected to an authoritarian, centralized, nationalistic, often racist government. Historically, fascists and National Socialists ('Nazis') such as Benito Mussolini (1883–1945) and Adolf Hitler (1889–1945) have sought and maintained power by ruthless acts of terror and genocide.

Realising utopia Across the political spectrum there are many ideologies which aim to transform society by force. Not all their adherents adopt terrorist methods, but many do, taking the oppressive nature of their opponents' regime as their justification. In resorting to terrorism are they not lowering themselves to the level of their opponents, or is it all a matter of degree?

The initial use of terror may trigger off a cycle of violence which cannot be halted once in motion, but surely terrorist tactics alienate potential supporters? Is it arrogant to impose one's utopia upon society by force rather than consent? On the other hand, would society ever have progressed without revolutionary views of the future? Which is more effective: the bullet or the ballot box?

Questions of land

Injustice is a breeding ground for conflict, and grievance over land, language and culture often provide a motive for terrorism. National boundaries are often the result of wars, treaties or colonial occupation: they may fail to take into consideration the traditions of the people who live in the area, or forcibly include ethnic groups within a nation state they do not wish to be a part of.

Self determination When one country extends its rule over other countries, sometimes settling them, it is said to pursue a policy of 'colonialism'. In our own century

> '. . . revolutionary action has wrested the erstwhile colonies away by the extortion of terror and civil disobedience . . .'
>
> Robert Taber in The War of the Flea, 1970

many movements have developed to resist colonialism and restore power to the local people.

Such wars of liberation have often been very brutal. In Algeria or in Kenya, for example, terror and atrocity were used by both fighters and colonists. Why did freedom fighters adopt terrorist tactics? Why did they not use constitutional means? The answer was that very often they had no constitutional means: they were deprived of effective political and economic power.

Why in their turn did the colonial powers themselves use terror? After all, it was they who claimed to have had a civilizing influence on the world. Was it that they regarded their subjects as inferior? Did their notion of democracy exclude some of their fellow human beings? The European colonists cited the freedom fighters' use of terror as a reason for excluding them from government. Was it not the colonists themselves who had created a climate of fear?

Homeless nations In some cases, international politics has deprived a whole people of a homeland. The Kurds are one example: their territory is occupied by Turkey, Iran and Iraq. This has led to a protracted conflict and misery.

Surely the answer to such injustice is to create a new homeland? This solution raises two problems. Firstly, there is no longer any habitable territory in the world which remains unsettled by other people. Secondly, culture, language and traditions make it difficult for a whole people to be transplanted and survive intact.

or language?

The creation of the state of Israel in 1948 encouraged the return of the much persecuted Jews to their ancient homeland, but in the process deprived the native Palestinian people of their own statehood. Was this a solution? The result has been decades of terrorism, and the emergence of such groups as the Jewish LEHI (or 'Stern Gang') and the Palestinian Black September. Warfare and mayhem now dominate the politics of the Middle East.

Home rule Groups who wish to withdraw from a nation state and rule themselves are known as 'separatist' or 'autonomist'. Groups who wish to see another territory incorporated within their own are known as 'irredentist'. Separatism and irredentism have led to some of the bloodiest conflicts of modern times, from Ireland to Biafra. French Canadians, Corsicans, Bretons, Scots, Welsh, Catalans, Basques, Canary Islanders, Eritreans, Baluchis and Tamils have all sought independence.

Separatist grievances are often aggravated by the fact that language or cultural traditions are proscribed or discounted. Are such matters worth bloodshed, or can they be defended in other ways? The nation state often blames separatist terrorism on narrow, aggressive nationalism. Are the states themselves not nationalistic? The pursuit of independence as a nation does not necessarily imply a narrow outlook, or aggression. Is self-determination as desirable an ideal for nations as it is for individuals?

At this funeral near San Sebastian, over 10,000 Basques came to mourn a suspected terrorist who died of wounds received in police custody. The Basques have their own language and culture; the terrorist organization ETA spearheads their movement for independence from Spain.

19

Killing for one's beliefs?

On 31 October 1984, the Indian prime minister Indira Gandhi was gunned down in New Delhi by two members of her own bodyguard. They were members of the Sikh religion, incensed by the government's treatment of their co-religionists. Troubles had come to a head when government troops attacked Sikh extremists occupying the Golden Temple in Amritsar; to many Sikhs this was sacrilege. In the hours following the assassination of Indira Gandhi, general terror erupted as Hindus sought out Sikh families and exacted revenge.

Defenders of the faith Most religions profess non-violence. The Old Testament of the Bible is clear enough: God's commandment to Moses was 'Thou shalt not kill.' In practice, however, acts of terror have been regularly committed in the name of religion: both Christianity and Islam have special words for a 'holy war' – 'crusade' and 'jihad'. The whole history of the crises that have rocked the Middle East centres upon the fact that Jerusalem is considered a holy city by three faiths – Christianity, Judaism and Islam.

In Lebanon, car bombs have been placed by both Christians and Muslims, whilst Jews patrol the streets in tanks. Religious sects such as Druze and Shiite seem to play an ever more important part as terror campaigns escalate. In Iran, the Ayatollah Khomeini advocates 'Islamic revolution' and gives his blessing to acts of terror and torture worthy of the regime he overthrew.

Religion and politics Are people who commit acts of terror in the name of religion insincere, or misguided in the application of their beliefs? Is Khomeini really concerned with spiritual matters, or with the politics of power? Or is such a divide, between politics and religion, artificial anyway? In South America, many Roman Catholic priests have sided with revolutionary forces against oppressive states. Are they betraying or carrying out their faith?

Why do not other believers do more to prevent terrorist activities? In Northern Ireland, where terrorism seems inextricably linked with religion, many Christians do work hard to build bridges between the Protestant community, which mostly wishes to retain links with the United Kingdom, and the Roman Catholic, which seeks union with the Republic. In such situations, are prayers enough? Are political initiatives of more practical use?

What part does religion really play in the major crises of the modern world? Some might argue that the conflict in Northern Ireland is the result of historical and economic forces rather than religion. Does the fact that different factions in Beirut might be Christian, Muslim or Jewish materially affect the problem? Is the quarrel ultimately a political struggle between Israel, Syria, and the great powers?

Philosophies of terror Atheistic philosophies rarely arouse popular passion in the same way as religions, but they may point to the climate of the times. 'Nihilists' for example, argue that there are no natural laws and no such thing as moral principles. Existentialist writers such as Albert Camus (1913–60) explored the implications of this in their work, and turned to revolt as the only meaningful human behaviour. The anarchist Mikhail Bakunin (1814–76) went one stage further: 'Let us put our trust in the eternal spirit which destroys and annihilates only because it is the source of life.' Would such a paradox make sense to a victim of terrorism?

'We have just enough religion to make us hate, but not enough to make us love one another.'

Jonathan Swift (1667-1745)

'They never miss the rosary every night.'

Joseph Maguire, H-block prisoner, Northern Ireland

The state as

W hat is meant by state terrorism? Do governments kidnap and murder in the same way as the terrorists they condemn? The evidence that they do is overwhelming. Even outwardly respectable governments use illegal methods to discredit, harm or even murder their opponents. Such activities are normally carried out in secret, but are sometimes openly acknowledged as policy by both executive and judiciary. They may also occur when state officers such as soldiers, jailers, police or secret agents, act without official sanction.

A survivor of Bergen-Belsen concentration camp delouses his clothes. The defeat of Germany's Nazis in 1945 revealed the depths of brutality to which a terrorist state can sink.

Torture and detention What tactics do governments adopt to terrify their opponents? One of the most common is torture: a 1984 report by Amnesty International suspected 66 countries of practising torture, despite the fact that it is outlawed by the United Nations, by the Geneva Convention and by many national constitutions. It may take the form of electric shocks, sensory deprivation, starvation or beatings and floggings. Mutilation is common, and in some countries, such as Pakistan, has been reintroduced as statutory public punishment for certain criminal offences.

Murder and abduction are widespread. In Argentina alone, thousands of people simply disappeared during the period of military rule which came to an end in 1983. One of the most disturbing examples of state terror is the internment of dissidents in mental hospitals, where they are treated with drugs. The USSR is one country which uses such treatment.

Agents of terror Do governments adopt terrorist tactics only against their own citizens? Colonel Muamar Qadhafi of Libya talks of 'exporting' terrorism. What does he mean? In practice, a small number of countries do sponsor terrorist attacks against expatriate opponents, and against the personnel of states it views as enemies. Some countries also give a refuge to terrorist groups with which they are in sympathy, and offer them training. The USA has accused Libya, Syria, Iraq and Iran of supporting terrorism in this way.

It might also be pointed out, however, that the secret services of almost all the major world powers also carry out acts that are illegal, and which endanger or take human life. Organizations such as the American CIA, the Soviet KGB, the South African BOSS and Israeli Mossad do not

a terrorist?

In July 1985 French secret service agents bombed this ship, the *Rainbow Warrior*, before it could take part in protests against French nuclear tests in the Pacific.

only spy on their enemies. They demoralize them by sabotage and terror.

In 1985, for example, the French secret service placed a bomb on a ship belonging to the ecological organization Greenpeace, peacefully at anchor in New Zealand. It was in the Pacific to protest at French nuclear testing in the region. A crew member was drowned.

Warfare or terrorism? Are world powers hypocritical in condemning acts of terrorism in others? In 1983, the US Navy shelled suburbs of Beirut, killing innocent civilians. An American hijack victim of June 1985 later said that he could understand his captors' desire for revenge. Is there a moral difference between such a shelling and a hijacking? Does the USA itself not seek revenge? Its 1986 air raid on Libya might be considered an example.

Could it be argued that the state is justified in using acts of terror against its opponents in order to protect the majority of its citizens? Is state terrorism simply a logical extension of formal warfare? In Japan, over 100,000 people were killed outright when on 6 August 1945, the US Airforce dropped a bomb on Hiroshima. Was this warfare or state terrorism?

'On the pretext of combating terrorism, Washington is itself committing one act of terrorism after another.'
Leonid Ponomarev, Soviet political commentator, TASS, July 1985

'We are capable of exporting terrorism to the heart of America.'
Colonel Muamar Qadhafi, Libyan leader

Terrorists as

In the Victorian era, some scientists believed one could tell a 'criminal' type by the shape of his or her head. Cesare Lombroso (1836–1909) was Professor of Forensic Medicine and Psychiatry at the University of Turin. He confidently asserted that 34 per cent of the anarchists in Turin were revealed as common criminals by their facial features alone. Fortunately nobody believes such nonsense today. We are still, however, confused as to how individuals can commit acts of terror that run counter to common codes of morality or honour. What makes someone become a terrorist?

Psychopaths or idealists? Are terrorists psychopaths? Some terrorists, as some murderers, are probably disturbed in one way or another. One such was Charles Manson: in 1969 he and his gang attempted to panic Californian white people into a racist uprising with a series of brutal murders. The obsessive bloodlust shown by the 'Family', as they were known, suggests that Manson was deranged.

Idealists, on the other hand, are often reluctant murderers. When faced with their victim, many fail to go through with the proposed act of terror. It is for this reason that many terrorist groups, such as the Provisional IRA, organize on military lines, subjecting their members to strict discipline and intimidation. The same psychological training that enables one young soldier to shoot another, is employed to make the terrorist able to kill a stranger. The victim is seen, not as an individual, but as an enemy group or class. Depersonalization of the conflict helps overcome natural feelings of revulsion.

Living with a feud Are terrorists people who have themselves been the victims of injustice or violence? Have they learned the lessons of terrorism from personal experience? Very often their lives have been traumatized by a tragedy for which they seek revenge. Perhaps it is significant that terrorists are often recruited from societies which traditionally accept blood feuding and the exactment of revenge in settlement of disputes. Often they have been born and raised in an aggrieved community which endorses violence; in the Palestinian refugee camps, or the slums of Belfast. Should we blame the individuals; or the society that produced them; or the wider issues that created such a society to start with?

Many terrorists in Europe and America, on the other hand, have not come from deprived or victimized backgrounds at all. Their education has led them to an analysis of society which makes them want to identify themselves with revolutionary causes. In this way, Germany's Baader-Meinhof group came to the aid of the Palestinian cause. Was their justification as valid as that of the Palestinians themselves?

Could it be that a desire for fame or notoriety motivates the individual terrorist? Terrorism certainly has its own mythology, and revolution is sometimes presented as a romance. Such dreams must be rapidly shattered by the reality of death and destruction. A terrorist *group* needs fame for its propaganda, but not for its individual members – hence the hoods and disguises in public.

Human nature? How then do we explain the psychology of the terrorist? Is it the result of criminality, mental illness, social background and indoctrination, education or idealism? Could it simply be a manifestation of human nature, a basic violence which is in all of us, but generally suppressed? And in the end does background or motivation in any way mitigate the immorality of a terrorist act?

individuals

Whose victory? Terrorist Ali Yussef, still defiant, lies shot by a bodyguard after a bomb attack on a Viennese synagogue in 1981.

'All terrorists must deny the relevance of guilt and innocence, but in doing so, they create an unbearable tension in their own souls, for they are in effect saying that a person is not a person.'

David Rapoport in Assassination and Terrorism, *1971*

The weaker sex?

On 6 September 1970, the PFLP (Popular Front for the Liberation of Palestine) assaulted four aircraft simultaneously at different airports. The London attack, on an El Al plane, failed: one of the Palestinians was killed, the other captured. Her name was Leila Khaled, and she came to symbolize the age of the hijacker.

Why did the press accord her such unprecedented publicity? Was it because she was a woman, traditionally regarded in society as the weaker sex, and presumed to be unaccustomed to violent action?

A road to power? If the public thought that acts of armed violence by women were something new, they were mistaken. Sophie Perovskaya took part in the assassination of the Russian Tsar, Alexander II, in 1872. The attack was organized by *Narodnaya Volya*, the 'People's Will' terrorist group, which was for a time led by a woman, Vera Figner. Women accounted for about a third of the group's membership.

> 'Women's participation in the [Russian] revolutionary movement which was of such immense value to its cause . . . yielded no benefits for the female half of the . . . people . . .'
>
> *Barbara Alpern Engel*

In ancient Rome and throughout history, women sometimes achieved political power for themselves or their husbands by organizing assassination or by poisoning their opponents. Why did they defy the role that society had defined for them in such a violent manner? Was it that, like many other groups that turn to terrorism, women formed a section of society that was deprived of institutional power?

At the start of the twentieth century, the international movement for women's suffrage adopted largely non-violent methods of protest, and countered state oppression with hunger strikes and acts of extreme civil disobedience. The emergence in the 1970s of female terrorists such as Leila Khaled, Ulrike Meinhof and Gudrun Ensslin coincided with a new international campaign to further women's rights and to promote the status of women in society. As an oppressed group, were women too going to use terror to defend their cause?

In fact, the new women terrorists were often fighting their battle on other issues, although sympathetic to the feminist struggle. Women had to make a choice between fighting for a patriotic or revolutionary cause, or concentrating upon that

Right Women try in vain to stop the rioting in Belfast, during the early days of the current troubles. The bus has become a barricade, and the street is littered with missiles.

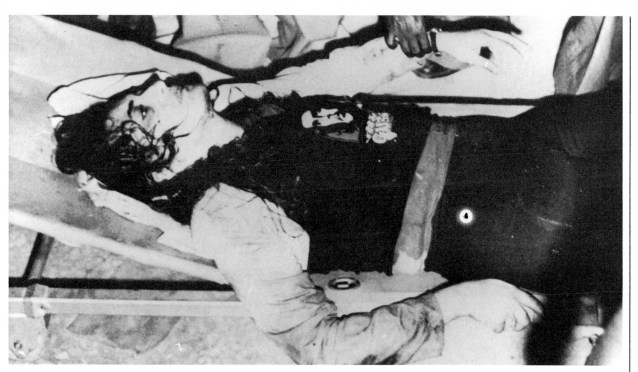

of women. All too often, revolutionary groups were male-dominated and unsympathetic to women. Turning to their own struggle, women more often chose to avoid violent tactics. After all, such tactics were symptomatic of the traditions that had denied them equality with men in the first place.

Promoters of peace or terror? In the troubles in Northern Ireland, women have played a key role as terrorists; ordinary women in the street too, have attempted to demoralize British troops by group action. In the 1980s there are as many women terrorists as ever.

In recent years, women have also taken the lead in developing non-violent protest and promoting peace. A women's movement for peace in Northern Ireland grew up in the 1970s, but failed amidst accusations of political naivety and self-interest. However the women's camp outside Greenham

A female terrorist is carried from the runway at Mogadiscio, Somalia. Her three collaborators were killed when West German commandos stormed the plane they had hijacked. On her chest is a portrait of Che Guevara.

> 'If our society had shown me a path other than violence, I would have taken it.'
>
> Vera Figner, anti-Tsarist terrorist, 1927

Common airbase, in England, has successfully focused international attention on protest against nuclear weapons.

Are women able to offer a dimension to political action which is different from that of men? Or is that belied by the extent of women's involvement in terrorist movements? Is the view of women as promoters of peace simply an extension of their traditional role, or is it a potential key to the solution of world crises? On the other hand, are governments run by women any less prone to state terrorism than those run by men?

On 29 October 1980, the China News Agency reported that terrorists had been responsible for an explosion in Beijing. The blast had gone off in the capital's busy railway station, killing 11 people and injuring 81. To the relatives and friends of the victims, the political motives of the bombers were probably irrelevant: they had suddenly lost the people they loved, and had their lives ruined in an instant. How can the murder of innocent civilians and children ever be acceptable to civilized people?

Questions of morality The moral issues surrounding terrorism are not always as clear as one might think. Is all human life equally sacred, or are there circumstances when murder is justifiable? On 20 July 1944, an attempt to blow up the Nazi leader Adolf Hitler, failed. If the tyrant had been killed, how many innocent lives would have been saved?

Is there a moral difference between murdering an innocent bystander and murdering the soldier of an oppressive army of occupation? Is there a difference between a soldier killing an enemy and a terrorist killing an enemy? Or between the murder of a child and the murder of an adult? Is *risking* human life as evil as *taking* human life?

Is bombing an empty building as morally reprehensible as the bombing of an armoured car? This question points to the value which our society places on life and on property. Do the criteria vary according to who the victim is, and who owns the property? Is a painting belonging to the queen protected with the same vigour as a caravan belonging to a gypsy? Do different societies have different values? Are these values affected by political, social or religious factors?

Politics and expedience Is the politician who orders troops to lay waste a foreign land morally superior to a terrorist? In his military writings, the Prussian field-marshal Count Helmuth von Moltke (1800–91) argued that war, being evil, was best got over with quickly: 'for that purpose all means are necessary', he wrote, 'not excluding the most blameworthy.' The moral contortions implicit in his argument might be echoed by the terrorists of today.

Who are the murderers? A Republican wall painting in Belfast compares Northern Ireland's prisons with concentration camps, and its police with the Nazis.

'Armed violence depresses and brutalises both the victim and the executioner.'

Nigel Young in New Internationalist, *January 1977*

wrong?

To kill or not to kill? In the end, the argument has to come down to whether it is permissible to kill at all. Many humanists, Buddhists, and Christians would agree that *no* circumstances justify the taking of life; the force of their argument has led to the abolition of capital punishment in many countries. According to Christian scripture, justice and revenge lie not in the hands of human beings, but of God; the terrorists have no right to appoint themselves judge and executioner. Might the terrorist not use the same argument to deny the validity of state judicial system?

Do theoretical arguments about morality affect the issue in practical terms? In a world where pure idealism is rare, do such arguments stand any chance of stopping the cycle of violence perpetrated by state and individual?

A widow visits a war cemetery after the Second World War. Is warfare a form of institutionalized terrorism, or a legitimate means of settling disputes?

'Vengeance is mine; I will repay saith the Lord.'
Romans 12: 19

Is there another way?

It seems to be true that in our society, violence breeds violence: state terror provokes reprisal by groups or individuals, and vice versa. Is there no way of achieving change without resorting to acts of violence?

Below Women at Greenham Common airbase, England. Non-violence may be a moral form of protest, but is it effective?

'Civil resistance is open and flexible, it subverts rather than confronts the forces of control.' *Nigel Young in* New Internationalist, *January 1977*

In a liberal social system, i.e. one that is neither revolutionary nor totalitarian, changes are intended to be carried out by a gradual process of reform. However, the people who resort to terror often believe that the reforms they can achieve through such a system are too slow, or insufficiently radical, to be effective. Terrorists rarely command sufficient support to carry out reform by democratic methods, or else they do not have input into a democratic system whereby reforms can be brought about.

Non-violence Are there alternatives to tactics of terror which can bring about change when democratic machinery fails? The general strike is one powerful means of protest, pressurizing the authorities economically, and demonstrating the extent of support for the cause in question. Mass demonstrations can also influence a government's policy. The British Campaign for Nuclear Disarmament (CND) pioneered methods of non-violent protest in the 1950s and 60s. They organized annual marches from London to the Atomic Weapons Research Establishment at Aldermaston. Members offered no resistance if arrested.

Non-violence had already been seen as an effective means of social change in India. Mohandas Gandhi (1869–1948) was hailed as *Mahatma* or 'great soul'. An ardent patriot, Gandhi wished to bring about the end of British rule in India. Instead of instigating a terror campaign, he organized 'civil disobedience' (in refusing to pay taxes, for example); he took part in protest marches; he refused food. Gandhi made the world aware of the Indian struggle for independence.

On the poster:
one little
cruise missile –
ten Nagasakis
Nagasakis
Nagasakis
Nagasakis
Nagasakis
Nagasakis
Nagasakis
Nagasakis

NO CRUISE
PERSHING II
SS 20s

START THE STEPS TO SURVIVAL

A mass demonstration by CND. After thirty years of demonstrations like this, has any British government taken notice of their demands?

Gandhi's use of moral example was of great influence. How effective was it in achieving practical aims? The British left India, but would they have done so if there were not other pressing reasons for doing so? Would Gandhi's tactics have worked against a totalitarian regime? Gandhi was himself assassinated. Does non-violence really have an effect?

Non-violent action can be successful if support for the movement is wide enough. Even the harshest tyrant finds it impossible to govern without any popular support. Non-violent action can gain public support in a way that terrorism cannot. Even if that support is not enough to remove a government, it can still be sufficient to force reform: the 1980 campaign by the trade union Solidarity in Poland is an example.

Breaking the law Civil disobedience obviously does not pose the same moral dilemmas as terrorism. However, it too involves breaking the law. Should all laws be respected equally, whether good or bad? Does democracy die in a society in which the rule of law has been abolished or eroded? Is the refusal to pay taxes on moral grounds just another criminal act, or is there a principle of natural justice which is greater than the statute book? And if there is, who decides what it is? Does not the terrorist also cite it to justify acts of violence?

'Power has never been willingly given up.'
Enver Carim in New Internationalist, January 1977

Strategies of fear

Opposite top Palestinian prisoners boarding a plane to freedom at Tel Aviv airport in November 1983. Do tactics of terror pay off in the world of international politics?

Many political campaigners reject terrorist tactics not only on the grounds of morality, but because they consider them to be counter-productive. Surely neither revolutionary groups nor governments can hope to gain popular support if they engage in murder and crime? Surely authorities are more likely to listen if they are reasoned with, rather than shot at?

Oppressors and martyrs In many cases, terrorists persist with their strategy because they do not want a dialogue in the first place. They aim instead to provoke a harsh reaction, so that the authorities may be seen to be oppressive. A bomb explodes, or a threat of terrorist action is phoned to a newspaper. The authorities use police or troops to investigate or restore order. Inevitably, some innocent people are confronted during the process: they become aggrieved and possibly even converted to the terrorists' cause. As terror escalates, a soldier or police officer might be panicked into overreacting. The authorities now seem to reveal themselves publicly as the oppressors they are made out to be, or perhaps are: they stand discredited.

Terrorists are aware that measures taken against them can create martyrs, and so promote their cause. The Easter Rising in Dublin in 1916 was suppressed by British troops. However, when the rebels were executed, such passions were aroused that the rebellion gained widespread support. The names of 1916 are still remembered in Ireland today, and groups such as the Irish National Liberation Army and the Provisional IRA promote new heroes to this pantheon, such as the hunger striker Bobby Sands.

Many revolutionaries and guerrillas take inspiration from martyrs to their cause, such as Ernesto 'Che' Guevara (1928–67):

executed by the Bolivian government, Guevara inspired a generation of revolutionaries. He himself dismissed tactics of terror as counter-productive. Martyrdom is, however, a force to be reckoned with in politics. In South Africa, the government's long imprisonment of activist Nelson Mandela, and the death of Steve Biko, only served to highlight the position of the Blacks, and to provide a focus for resistance to the injustice of *apartheid*.

Of course martyrdom is a double-edged weapon. The victims of terrorist attacks may themselves achieve sympathy for their government or cause, and so achieve a very different effect than that originally intended.

Ends and means A frequent aim of terrorists is to commit an act of violence and then pretend that it was done by another group, or by the government, and so discredit them. This is part of a general policy of destabilization. Other tactics have more immediate goals. Assassination can bring about a change of government; a kidnapping can raise ransom money; a hijacking can release prisoners. When, in the summer of 1985, 40 Americans were held hostage in Lebanon, it effectively expedited the release of hundreds of Shiite Moslem prisoners illegally held in Israel.

The 1881 Anarchists' Congress in London called for 'propaganda by the deed'. Do terrorist strategies, adopted by government, group or individual, work as *propaganda*? And to whose advantage? If a liberation movement resorts to terror, as opposed to guerrilla warfare, it may expedite its immediate ends: but will people trust it with eventual government? However successful they are, are terrorists only digging their own graves? Do their ideals die with their victims?

Opposite bottom Armed French police frisk a Corsican autonomist after a hostage-taking incident in January, 1980. Do terrorists aim to provoke the state into a show of strength?

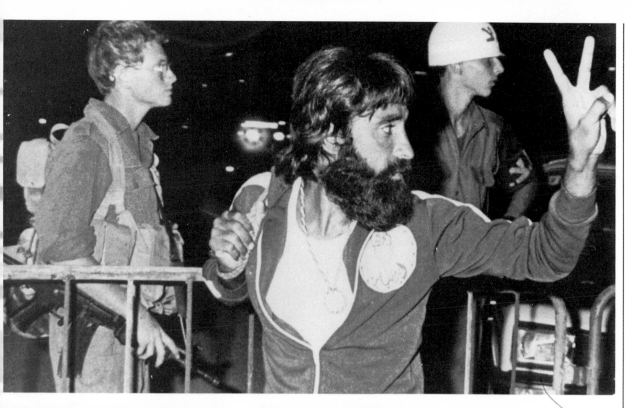

'We sincerely believe that terrorism is of negative value, that it by no means produces the desired effect, that it can turn people against a revolutionary movement . . .'

Ernesto 'Che' Guevara (1928-67)

'. . . the threat [of bombing the 1969 investiture of the Prince of Wales] meant that the Special Branch would pressure Welsh people, and Welsh people would turn against them.'

John Jenkins, leader of Mudiad Amddiffyn Cymru, jailed 1970

Death: the ultimate terror?

O n 17 February 1978, incendiary devices set a Belfast restaurant ablaze. The restaurant was crowded, and children were among the diners. Twelve people were killed, and 30 injured. The Provisional IRA was responsible. Terrorists must learn to live with violent death: it is their ultimate weapon, and quite probably the method of their own end.

Their victims are many each year: political and religious leaders, soldiers, police, collaborators, informers, rivals and random innocent civilians. There are victims of state terror too: political dissidents, the poor and hungry, enemy civilians, peaceful demonstrators. Tragically, it is the death of innocent members of the public that causes maximum terror, so serving the terrorist well.

Murderous technology Terrorists have developed a deadly arsenal: bombs are still the prime cause of deaths. They are left in station lockers, litter bins and shops. They are sent through the post, so designed that they kill or maim whoever tries to open the packet. They are left in parked cars with timing devices, or fixed underneath vehicles so that they explode as the driver turns the ignition. The British Conservative MP Airey Neave, for example, was killed by a car bomb in March 1979; it had been placed by the INLA (Irish National Liberation Army). In 1983, over 500 people throughout the world were killed by bombs planted in cars.

Explosive devices often take the form of booby traps, to be triggered off by police or troops during their investigations. Often a second bomb is timed to explode once the security forces have arrived on the scene. Sophisticated timing devices and modern electronics have assisted bombers in their tasks.

Italian terrorists escape, after a robbery becomes a murder. The Red Brigades later demanded the release of these two men from jail, in return for the life of kidnapped ex-premier Aldo Moro.

'Any man's death diminishes me, because I am involved in mankind . . .'
*John Donne
(1571-1631)*

The tragic reality: a young woman lies on the pavement after a synagogue in Paris is bombed by anti-Israeli terrorists.

Assassins of public figures have also been aided by modern technology, for example by high-precision rifles with telescopic or night sights. In an extraordinary case in 1978, a Bulgarian defector was assassinated in London, poisoned by a tiny pellet from an umbrella-gun. Incidents of assassination increased nearly seventy-fold in the 1970s.

The effect of modern technology is to distance the killer from the victim: Brutus no longer has to meet Caesar face to face. Is this the coward's way out? Does the means of death affect the end result?

How we see death The victims of terrorist attacks are often Europeans and Americans.

Is this only because they belong to rich and powerful nations? Could it be that these nations are more vulnerable, because their attitudes to death differs from those of other societies? In the west today, death is a taboo subject, which society does its best to conceal. Bereavement is traumatic, and death the ultimate terror. In many poorer countries, however, everyday life is a struggle: people are inured to death by starvation or disease, and fatalistic about disaster. Are acts of terror less effective when carried out against such people? Is an obsessive fear of death the chink in the armour of the world's most powerful nations?

Hostages and

On 16 March 1978, Italian politician and former premier Aldo Moro was ambushed on his way to parliament. Armed terrorists of the Red Brigades gunned down his escorts and abducted him to a secret location. For nearly two months, Italy was in a state of total confusion as the government received demands and statements from the kidnappers, and pleas from the victim. The police seemed powerless. Eventually, the terrorists announced that Moro had been 'sentenced to death': his body was found on 9 May. His killers were finally jailed in 1983.

Bargaining by menace Kidnapping is a tactic terrorist groups have borrowed from the world of organized crime. By taking away a person's liberty, the kidnappers

'The secret of surviving in these conditions is to live for the day . . . Disappointment is so crippling.' Moorhead Kennedy, former US hostage in Iran

hope to bargain, blackmail, or protect their interests in some other way. They might seek to extort money from the victim's family or firm, demand the release of political prisoners or other terrorists from custody, or simply to remove the victim from the public stage at a crucial moment.

The victim is normally a prominent person, such as a general or a judge: Hanns-Martin Schleyer, kidnapped by supporters of the Baader-Meinhof group in 1977, was a leading industrialist. Are such victims selected because of their wealth or bargaining power? Or is it because terrorists consider them guilty in the first place? Certainly, terrorists of some political persuasions would view them as collaborators with, or pillars of, a hostile state or social order.

Is depriving somebody of their liberty more defensible than harming or killing them? Kidnap attempts do in fact anyway often result in the murder of the victim. Terrorists such as the Red Brigades, consider such murder to be 'execution' and the kidnapping itself as 'imprisonment'. Does such a comparison make a valid political point, or is the terrorists' summary justice no different from that of a lynch mob?

Right A hostage crisis in Barcelona, Spain. A bank employee is held at gunpoint as government negotiators enter the central bank.

kidnapping

Embassies under siege Foreign diplomats have always been prime targets for kidnaps and hostage-taking. Perhaps the most famous such incident happened in 1979 when Islamic revolutionary guards seized the US embassy in Tehran. They demanded that the former ruler, the Shah, should be returned to Iran for trial. Fifty-two hostages were held for a total of 444 days, whilst military rescue bids failed. Tactics of terror succeeded in confounding the most powerful nation on earth.

In 1980, no less than 40 embassies were besieged worldwide. By 1982, statisticians reckoned that 54 per cent of all terrorist victims that year were diplomats. Embassies were clearly vulnerable outposts, and therefore a prime target for the terrorists.

Ambassadors are such important figures that governments are bound to take some note of the terrorists' demands. Furthermore, international relations are delicate: the possibility that secret documents might be discovered on embassy property, or that the host country may be placed in a politically embarrassing position, only aids the terrorists' cause. In the world of modern communications, one might wonder why embassies are still there: could they not be dispensed with?

In striking at embassies, are terrorists undermining the foundations of international understanding? Surely diplomats assist in the dialogue between nations that is the key to the solution of international crises?

A welcome in Frankfurt, West Germany, for 39 Americans held hostage by Shiite Moslems in Beirut during July 1985.

The hijackers

The word 'hijack' first came into widespread use during the 1920s. In the USA, public consumption of alcohol was prohibited, so racketeers vied with one another to supply liquor to illicit bars. Lorries and their loads were often stolen in transit – or 'hijacked'.

In the 1960s, the term took on an altogether more sinister meaning, for the cargoes being hijacked were human. Terrorists were seizing aircraft and forcing pilots to fly to a new destination. Passengers were held at gunpoint, while their captors issued demands to the authorities. Sometimes hijacking was used as a means of escape from a hostile country, or a dangerous situation.

Today, a hijacking takes place somewhere in the world nearly every week. Landing, refuelling and negotiation are fraught with danger, a nightmarish battle of nerves between airline staff, air traffic controllers, passengers and terrorists. By the summer of 1986, fear of terrorism in the air was already resulting in a decline of tourist traffic.

Vulnerability Why has air travel been disrupted in this way? It is of course vulnerable by its very nature. When the pilot has a gun at his or her head, anything can happen. All kinds of counter-measures have been tried. Airport security has been improved, with X-ray and metal-detecting equipment now a routine, and 'sniffers' of explosives being introduced. There is here a problem that constantly arises when terrorism is on the increase: the restriction of personal liberty.

Hijackings create all kinds of problems. How for example can food and drink be sent to the victims? Here, meals are being prepared for hostages held during the Dutch train siege of 1977.

A balance has to be struck between freedom of movement and security. Most passengers are grateful for the detailed searches, but some methods are more worrying: an armed guard on a plane might result in a stray bullet depressurizing the cabin.

Airline pilots have threatened to boycott airports where security is lax, and international conventions have discussed the issue, at Tokyo, Den Haag and Montreal. Traditional enemies such as Cuba and the USA, have come to agreement on the issue. And yet even so, the hijackings continue.

Is there no more effective solution or deterrent? Sometimes full-scale commando raids have been carried out on hijacked planes at airports. In 1977, a West German *Grenzschütz* force stormed a Lufthansa plane in Mogadiscio, the Somali capital. Its Palestinian hijackers were demanding the release from prison of West German and Turkish supporters. The hijackers were killed or wounded, and all 86 passengers freed. However in 1985, at Valletta, Malta, there was rather a different outcome. An Egyptian *Saiqa* commando group led an assault on an Egyptair Boeing 737 hijacked by terrorists of the Abu Nidal faction: 60 passengers died in the fighting. Was such loss of life worthwhile? The pilot later argued that there had been no alternative to the action, tragic as it had been.

In 1985, the US government developed a new strategy: hijacking the terrorists themselves. Although such action received popular support, it disturbed America's allies: was breaking international law the only way to prevent international law being broken?

Aircraft are not the only form of transport liable to hijacking. A school bus was hijacked in Djibouti in 1976; and trains in the Netherlands in 1975 and 1977. In 1985, the Italian liner *Achille Lauro* was hijacked during an Egyptian cruise.

The end of a hijack: Amal militia blow up a 727 jet on the runway at Beirut in June 1985. Fortunately, the passengers had already been taken off the plane.

> 'Hijacking is a crime . . . When cruelty is inflicted on innocent people, it discredits whatever cause . . .' Ronald Reagan, US President, June 1985

For the terrorist, hijack remains one of the riskiest enterprises, with a high risk of capture and death, and the need for a safe haven for landing. Despite this, it remains common, for it achieves its objectives surprisingly often. This could be because it exploits twin fears – the death of innocent people, and the loss of millions of pounds worth of property – and thus achieves maximum publicity.

Criminal

hree days before Christmas in 1971, a West German policeman was shot dead as a group of terrorists carried out a bank raid in Kaiserslautern. Bank raids are a common method of funding terrorist or other revolutionary groups, from South America to Northern Ireland.

> ## 'To steal from the rich is a sacred and religious act.'
> Jerry Rubin, 1960s Yippie leader in USA

How do terrorists square such methods, normally associated with non-political crime, with their ideals? The defence that banks are capitalism's front line, and part of a repressive economic system, may have

its own logic. Again, however, innocent lives are risked: is a bank clerk to be blamed for taking a job at a bank?

Mayhem Robbery is not the only such tactic however. The terrorists' need to enforce discipline and prevent information being passed to the authorities, has led to the use of methods reminiscent of the Mafia: intimidation, extortion, protection rackets, grievous bodily harm, blackmail, torture and maiming. Crippling victims by 'knee-capping' has been one of the cruellest practices in Northern Ireland. If terrorists participate in such activities, are they at all different from common criminals? Is a cause which can accept such practices worth fighting for?

Gangland killings in the United States: a Mafia bodyguard lies dead. Many politically motivated terrorists use the same criminal methods as gangsters.

tactics?

State terrorism is often just as sadistic, and can be extremely terrifying. Oppressive governments use every criminal method, from petty violence to systematic torture. Special squads are set up to harrass and murder opponents. In such countries, state officials are very often themselves involved in organized crime, or are prepared to turn a blind eye to criminal activities by others.

Crimes against property Much terrorist activity, as in the criminal world, is directed against property alone. This is often motivated by a genuine desire to avoid bloodshed. Such tactics are also sometimes adopted because the campaigners see society as placing overmuch value on property: they are hitting the system where it hurts. Are

such attacks against property 'terrorist'? Certainly their aim is to increase fear and destroy morale.

Is an arsonist with a cause to be treated as a political activist or as a malicious fire-raiser? Since 1979, over a hundred empty holiday homes have been burned down in

> *'Property is theft.'*
> Pierre Joseph Proudhon (1809-1865)

Wales. The purchase of second homes, largely by people living and working in England, has led to the depopulation of many parts of rural Wales. Undoubtedly, some people have been dissuaded from buying second homes as a result of the campaign, which intensive police operations have failed to halt. But can the arsonists be sure that they will not endanger human life in such an attack, even if inadvertently? Are such acts likely to escalate into more extreme acts of terrorism? Or are they a conscious substitute for such acts?

Sabotage is another technique favoured by terrorists and guerrillas. The aim of sabotage is to hamper one's opponent by disrupting work and essential supplies. The destruction of factory machinery and the blowing up of a railway line, serve as practical demonstrations that the authorities cannot maintain control. Again, there is potential danger to human life. But is the vandal who throws an obstruction on to a railway track any less culpable than a saboteur?

In 1984, militant animal liberationists claimed to have poisoned retail foodstuffs in an attempt to dissuade the public from buying the products of companies they accused of animal experimentation. Hoax or not, this novel kind of sabotage hits hard at a consumer society. How should the perpetrators be penalized? As terrorists or as criminals?

Left The bank raid is one way in which terrorists fund their activities. Here, a 1974 raid on a San Francisco bank by a group known as the SLA included the kidnapped heiress Patty Hearst, who later pleaded that she was acting under duress.

Using the media?

During the Lebanon hostage crisis of June 1985, the American captives were led before the television cameras for a press conference by Amal leader, Nabih Berri. The crisis was thus brought into the living rooms of millions of ordinary Americans, and the hijackers' cause received publicity.

> 'We must try to find ways to starve the terrorist and the hijacker of the oxygen of publicity on which they depend.'
>
> Margaret Thatcher, British Prime Minister

There is increasing concern that the media's never-ending quest for sensation plays into the hands of the terrorists. Do television news reports accord the same importance to non-violent protest as they do to acts of violence? Are the hijackers playing to the gallery? Could it be that television reporting of terrorism sets an example, and encourages further acts of terror?

The power of television Almost every individual terrorist or group uses the press and television to promote their cause or disseminate fear. But then do not states (and not just overtly oppressive ones) manipulate the media in their turn, and use them to lay a smoke-screen over their activities? It is surely no coincidence that the sharp rise in terrorist incidents in recent decades, has taken place at the same time as the growth of television as the prime news medium. Many people believe that it was television that turned American opinion against the Vietnam War prior to 1973. For the first time, the violence of warfare was being seen by the general public at first hand. Television is a powerful political weapon.

A duty to report? Are the media to blame? Surely they have to report events as they happen, and so play a vital part in a free society? In 1985, the South African regime accused foreign journalists of being respon-

American hostages in the Lebanon are brought to a press conference by their captors. Do terrorists rely on the media to further their cause?

'You can't be a revolutionary today without a colour television set – it's as important as a gun.'

Jerry Rubin, 1960s Yippie leader in USA

At a secret press conference, members of the Basque ETA organization remain hooded. Do the press have a duty to report such events?

sible for the increasing number of terrorist incidents and outbreaks of violence in the Republic. Many journalists responded by saying that it was political injustice that created rioting, not television cameras. Certainly, there was no sudden end to the troubles after reporting facilities were restricted.

Is censorship of news ever permissible in a free society? Is it permissible during wartime or during an emergency? Can any news reporting be objective, or is it always coloured by opinion or attitude? In the summer of 1985, the governors of the BBC, a supposedly independent body, bowed to pressure from the then Home Secretary, and decided not to broadcast in its existing form a documentary film about the troubles in Northern Ireland, called *At the Edge of the Union*. The BBC later announced that the film would be shown at a later date, but journalists working for both the BBC and ITV (the commercial network) went on strike. Were they right to protest?

The tabloid press Perhaps the chief problem with media coverage of terrorism is the way in which popular newspapers trivialize events. Little attempt is made to examine issues in depth. Terrorists are derided, but at the same time glamourized with nicknames taken from novels or films: 'Carlos', Ilyich Ramirez Sanchez, is dubbed 'The Jackal' or 'the world's most wanted terrorist'.

After the *Achille Lauro* incident in 1985, the US military intercepted the ship's hijackers by forcing down a plane in which they were travelling. The New York *Daily News* ran a headline 'We bag the bums'. The fight against terrorism is ill served by turning it into a war comic.

How do terrorists

How do terrorists avoid detection? The entire resources of the police and the military may be directed against them, and yet they still survive.

> *Moscow . . . has developed more purpose . . . in its manipulation of this international terrorist movement.'* Leader in The Times, June, 1985

Yasir Arafat, leader of the PLO, takes the salute. A military structure helps enforce discipline and maintain morale.

Like most revolutionary organizations, the larger terrorist groups favour a 'cell' structure. Each cell or unit consists of just three or four members, who do not know members of other cells. One member acts as a link with other groups, but only the commanding body has an overall picture of the structure. This system ensures that if a member is arrested and interrogated, he or she will only be able to pass on limited information. The success of this structure was demonstrated between 1954 and 1962 by the Algerian FLN (*Front de Libération Nationale*) in their struggle against the French colonists.

Military ranks are sometimes used to encourage an equation of the organization with a regular army. The Provisional IRA is divided into 'brigades', each of which is made up of 'battalions'. When secrecy is jeopardized, authority may be reinforced by intimidation and murder. Most terrorist organizations are authoritarian in their internal structure.

Community roles Some terrorist groups enjoy a certain degree of support from the community in which they are based, even if their operations are carried out in hostile territory. The Basque separatist organization ETA is one example, and the Palestinian groups too – although the latter have often been harrassed by the countries in which their refugee camps are based. Others, such as West Germany's terrorist cells, have been supported by minorities of political sympathizers, but not received widespread backing from a class or community.

Sometimes a purely political programme or front organization is sponsored, to win support for the cause and present a case to the public by more generally acceptable means. Provisional *Sinn Fein*, for example, is the political wing of the Provisional IRA, putting up candidates for elections, and

organize?

working within the community from which they seek support. This poses a problem for a UK government. Should it encourage and formally endorse such democratic developments, and open dialogue? Or would such a policy mean letting in terrorism by the back door?

> '. . . the organization was elastic, based on factors of population and terrain.'
>
> Tom Barry, IRA leader in the 1920s

Arms purchase is partly paid for by robbery and extortion, partly by private donations from sympathizers, partly by fundraising through legal front-organizations. One such is NORAID, which raises money for Northern Ireland amongst Republican sympathizers in the USA.

International collaboration Perhaps the most remarkable development in modern terrorist organizations has been the establishment of international links between various groups, between separatists and leftists, and between different fascistic organizations.

In 1972, terrorists of the Japanese Red Army (*Sekigun*), who had trained with the PLO (Palestinian Liberation Organization) in Libya, killed 24 travellers and injured 76 at Tel Aviv's Lod Airport, in Israel. In the 1975 attack on OPEC in Vienna, the terrorists were Venezuelan, Lebanese, Palestinian and West German.

From Ireland to Canada to South America, links are made, formal or informal; information is exchanged, and joint training organized. Sympathetic countries such as Libya, provide a common forum. Nevertheless, terrorist alliances, like any alliance, are liable to strain and differences of opinion over tactics or ideology. Many are rivals.

Fighting against terrorism

How is terrorism to be checked? Is it possible to counter the effectiveness of the terrorists without limiting human rights and inhibiting liberty? What methods are at society's disposal?

Surveillance and detection are the chief weapons used by the authorities against individual terrorists or groups. Incidents are monitored and evaluated, and information is stored on computer and exchanged internationally. Security arrangements are intensified: prominent people are guarded, their mail is checked, public places are searched, and the public warned to beware and report any unusual happenings.

Psychologists investigate the mental tensions experienced by hijackers or people under siege, and advise police when to act. Techniques are developed for defusing bombs or exploding them by remote control. One British firm organizes courses for British businessmen who travel abroad: they are taught self-defence, and briefed on the best way to deal with a situation in which they are liable to be hijacked or taken hostage.

Is there a danger that increased surveillance and counter-terrorist activity, whilst deterring acts of terrorism, will lead to a 'big-brother' state? Is such a response, paradoxically, giving in to terrorism, in that traditional freedoms are eroded, thus creating in turn a terrorist state? Or is it a practical necessity, to protect human life?

How can state terror itself be countered? One technique developed by organizations such as Amnesty International is to collect data from trustworthy sources and then publish it. In this way, the attention of the international community is focused on abuses of power, and formal commissions may be established to monitor human rights in any one country. Tours of inspection, lobbying and appealing to the UN, can all add to international pressure for reform.

An anti-tank cannon and other weapons siezed by the FBI are put on public display in New York. They were destined for the Provisional IRA.

A SAS commando storms the Iranian embassy in London during the hostage crisis of May 1980. Such action can bring a swift conclusion, but at a great risk to life.

Meeting violence with violence? When a terrorist attack is already in process, extreme measures may be taken. Special commando squads are trained to attack at high speed: in the USA they are part of the Army Delta Force; in West Germany part of the *Grenzschütz.* On 5 May 1980, gunmen were holding hostages at the Iranian embassy in London. Elite troops of the British Special Air Services (SAS) stormed their way into the building, and successfully released 19 hostages. Such missions are fraught with danger, in that they endanger human life and raise the stakes in delicate situations. Is there perhaps another danger: that the glorification of the heroism involved might encourage the view that it is possible to solve the problem of terrorism by military action alone?

Terror is sometimes met by terror, with horrific methods employed: torture, interrogation, and military reprisals, against sympathizers or even innocent people. During the Second World War, German occupying forces would shoot whole villages, in retaliation for sabotage or action by partisans.

All response to terrorism, whether judicial, military or terrorist in itself, runs the risk of uniting the opposition, creating martyrs, and offending principles of morality. Should a government risk military tactics before it has exhausted diplomatic approaches, or other methods such as economic sanctions? Are oppressive measures justified against oppressive people? Did the US attack on Tripoli in 1986 achieve anything that political methods have not done?

'None of the options [of retaliation] are appealing.' George Church in Time magazine, June, 1985

Counter measures may contain the problem, but in a superficial way; buying more weapons will not get to the root of the problem in Northern Ireland or the Middle East.

Terror and the law

One of the chief weapons used by the state to combat terrorism is the law: terrorists must be brought to justice. The difficulty arises, however, in deciding *who's* justice. Terrorists are already outlaws who deny the legitimacy of the judicial system that

'Where laws end, tyranny begins.' *William Pitt (1708-1778)*

tries them. Some deny the right of *any* court to try them; all states, of course, assert their own legitimacy, and normally reject any notion that the terrorist is a 'political' prisoner, different from a common criminal.

Questions of status To the terrorist, the fight for recognition as a special case is crucial, for in granting special status, a government is to some extent admitting their opponents' right to action. This issue was at the centre of bitter protest by prisoners in Northern Ireland, which led to the murder of warders, hunger strikes, and the so-called 'dirty protest', in which H-block prisoners refused to wear prison clothes and plastered their cells with their own excrement.

Legislation Northern Ireland is an example of the legal confusion which can be caused by terrorism. Under what circumstances, if any, should basic civil rights be suspended? In 1972, by accepting the proposals of the Diplock Report, the British Parliament admitted that its legal system could not withstand terrorist pressure; it was prepared to suspend traditional legal rights within a territory that it held to be part of the United Kingdom. An 'extra-judicial process' was to be introduced.

Trial by jury was the chief casualty. For certain offences, the accused were no longer assumed to be innocent unless proved otherwise: the 'onus of proof' now lay with the defendant. Confessions, informers and detention became features of Northern Ireland's legal system.

Do extraordinary circumstances demand extraordinary measures, as in wartime? Opponents of the Northern Ireland (Emergency Provisions) Act, 1973, maintained that the legislation, far from opposing terrorism, was giving in to it. Should the legal system not stand by the courage of its own convictions? If justice is not seen to be done, are grievances only exacerbated?

The Prevention of Terrorism Act of 1974 was admitted at the time to be 'draconian',

Right Members of the Italian Red Brigades stand trial in a Milan courtroom. The defendants are barred inside a steel cage and guarded by *carabinieri.*

'The only hope of restoring the efficiency of criminal courts of law in Northern Ireland is to deal with terrorist crimes by using an extra-judicial process.'

The Diplock Report, 1972

FEMMES ET MÈRES
DE PRISONNIERS RÉPUBLICAINS
IRLANDAIS
NOUS DÉNONÇONS
LA TORTURE DANS
LES PRISONS ET LES
VIOLENCES CONTRE
LA POPULATION

LONG KESH

and yet it has been repeatedly endorsed by the British Parliament. Its far-reaching police powers have resulted in nearly 6,000 arrests up to 1985. Its effectiveness may be gauged from the fact that as a result of those arrests, only 17 people were charged with offences related to the Act, and 311 on other charges. Might it not be said that the extension of police powers without achieving the prevention of terrorism, is counter-productive? Might this really be the Encouragement of Terrorism Act?

The law at risk Throughout the world, terrorists have placed the judiciary in a dilemma. Prisons which are already crowded, have been pushed beyond their limits. For the 1975 trial of the Baader-Meinhof group in West Germany, the authorities had to build a special stronghold outside Stuttgart, at vast expense. Judges need armed bodyguards. Trials against Italy's Red Brigades became farcical, with the defendants caged in court.

Clearly, the legal system is one of the most vulnerable parts of any liberal society. How are its interests best served?

In 1977, mothers and wives of Republican prisoners travelled to Paris. They wore blankets like those of the prisoners, who were refusing to wear prison clothes as part of their endeavours to receive 'political' status.

In the public

P̲ublic attitudes to terrorism depend upon the nature of the act involved, and the political relationship between the terrorist, victim and observer. Reports in the newspapers and on television can also play an important part in influencing public opinion, as can propaganda, whether issued by the terrorists or their opponents. In almost any group, the murder of innocent bystanders arouses revulsion and demands for harsh retribution: understandably, for the public is in the front line.

> 'They should shoot the guys.' *American interviewed on the street, 1985*

Public pressure Such killings, and hijackings or kidnappings of compatriots, result in public calls for action by the politicians. In reality, the political actions which can be taken are often very limited.

During the 1979–80 crisis in which Americans were held hostage in Iran, US President Jimmy Carter was severely criticized for his mishandling of the affair. When Ronald Reagan succeeded to the presidency, however, he too was faced with hostage crises, and discovered in turn that his options were few.

There is a real danger that public opinion, which has been inadequately informed by a sensationalist press, will stampede the politicians into hasty and ill-considered action. Politicians seeking re-election may find it easier to placate the crowd at their heels with military reprisal or harsh legislation, than to steer a less spectacular and more diplomatic course.

The basis of power In the end, however, it must be remembered that it is the public which wields ultimate power: as well as making or breaking their political representatives, they can make or break the terror-

eye

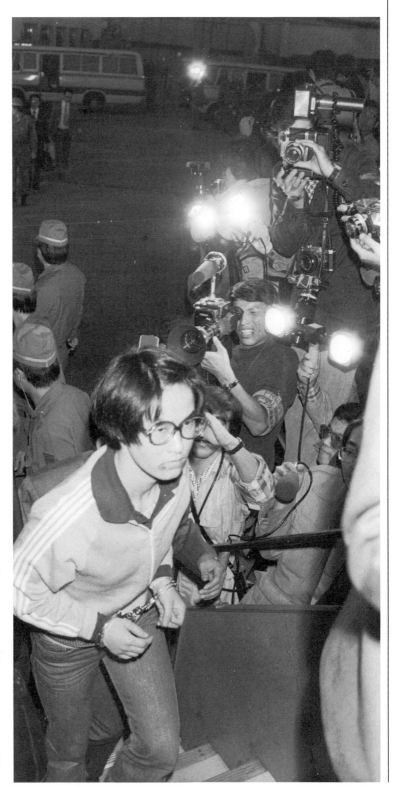

ists. Both Loyalist and Republican terrorists in Northern Ireland may receive support from their immediate followers, but their broader aim must be to win over public opinion in Britain, the Irish Republic and the world at large: tactics of terror are the chief obstacle to this happening.

This having been said, there can be little doubt that terrorists have in the past succeeded in focusing world attention on an issue. The PFLP activities were universally condemned, but it cannot be denied that they made the Palestinian cause known to the public in western Europe and America.

Armed struggles which avoid methods of terror inevitably receive more international sympathy, although it should be borne in mind that political opponents of such struggles nearly always accuse the guerrillas of being terrorists, regardless of whether they are or not. During independence struggles, the support of peasant societies with strong traditions of loyalty, have not only assisted the guerrillas, but have gained them international sympathy. They are clearly seen to have the support of their community.

State versus public Just as the public has to be the ultimate judge of individual terrorists or groups, so it must be the judge of state terrorism.

Within a totalitarian state, social conformity is considered to be a virtue, and the climate is hostile to any protest. Nevertheless, even the most violent state cannot survive without the cooperation of some of its citizens. Again, international opinion must be mobilized, and open government encouraged: only an informed public is able to make judgements.

But above all, whether the state is totalitarian or liberal, the citizen must listen, learn, and arrive at an independent view: terrorism thrives on bigotry.

Society as

Since the current troubles in Northern Ireland began in 1969, well over 3,000 people have been murdered in the province. During the last twenty years we have all become accustomed to public grief: on television we see outrages, atrocities and pain.

Can we really understand how the relatives of the victims really feel? Are we able to imagine ourselves in the position of someone who has been crippled for life as the result of a random explosion? Or do we become inured to violence by its relentless exposure? Before we sanction violence in political argument or cheer on an invading army, we should perhaps consider the full

> 'What they did was wrong. I don't forgive it, but I don't feel resentful or bitter, and I hold nothing against them.'
>
> Moorhead Kennedy, former US hostage in Iran

implications in human terms: how would we feel if the victim was one of our own family?

The affect on society Could it be that increased terrorism has, in a way, made us *all* the victims? A society in which terrorist attacks are frequent becomes frightened, close and often callous. Surely civilization can only flourish when such conditions are reversed? On the other hand, could it be that it is only a society in which civilization has already broken down that produces terrorism? Does the blame really lie with self-interested government, with economic exploitation and repression?

Whatever the cause, the result has been widespread demoralization. People no longer feel in control of their own destinies: they feel powerless to prevent the rising tide of violence. And yet that will only be stemmed, if people are prepared to participate in society and work for political solutions. Every unthought response or shrug of indifference only serves to compound the problem.

Terrorist groups often acclaim the perpetrators of random acts of violence as heroes. Surely such acts run counter to the whole notion of heroism, the belief in a fair fight with an enemy, face to face? National armies, of course, play the same game and have long abandoned such ideals, bombing civilians with a clear conscience. Is it perhaps a hypocritical ideal to aspire to anyway, if the end result – death – remains the same? Perhaps so, and yet here too the ideology of terrorism seems to impinge upon society at large. Individuals fail to take personal responsibility for their actions. Surely a prerequisite of civilized behaviour, even in a society which has no generally agreed moral code, is that the individual must work out a personal code of morality, based on experience?

Some people argue that if each individual in society lived by such a moral code, there would be no need for political action. The problem with this argument is that cooperation is clearly necessary for social organiz-

the victim?

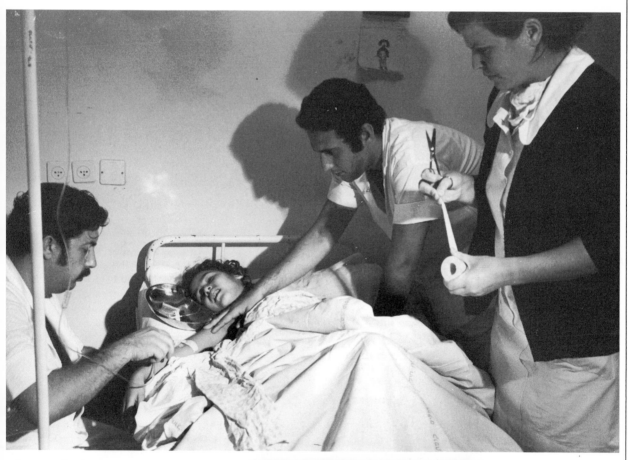

ation, and that necessitates individual compromise.

Society, the target and victim of terrorist action, must respond with optimism and the political determination to deal justly with the root causes of terrorism. Resignation and denial of personal involvement can only encourage an endless cycle of violence.

'A man that studieth revenge keeps his own wounds green.'
Francis Bacon (1561-1626)

A young child, victim of an attack by Palestinian guerrillas, is treated by Israeli doctors.

Coping with an emergency

W hen violence is met with violence, there is little evidence of humanity in action. On all sides are bombed out buildings, blazing fires, or dead bodies: a chilling desolation. Fortunately, both for the victims and for humanity as a whole, there are people prepared to risk their own lives in the relief of human misery. As a society, do we give these people the recognition they deserve? Do we acknowledge the debt we owe them?

Emergency services In the front line are workers for the fire service. They have to learn how to cope with horrors normally associated with total warfare: collapsing buildings, burned bodies, fire bombs and booby traps. Some terrorists turn upon the emergency services as part of the social order they wish to disrupt. Fire engines have on occasions been attacked by angry mobs. Similar dangers are experienced by ambulance drivers, who must retrieve victims of terror from violent situations, sometimes even under gunfire, and offer comfort to people in pain or distress.

Police forces, too, if they are not partisan or themselves agents of terror, can play an important part in the relief of suffering and the peaceful resolution of the confrontation. More than any of the emergency services, the police are open to attack and violence. The April 1984 murder of WPC Yvonne Fletcher, during a siege at the Libyan People's Bureau in London, aroused massive public sympathy.

The most dangerous job of all is that of bomb disposal experts. Whenever possible,

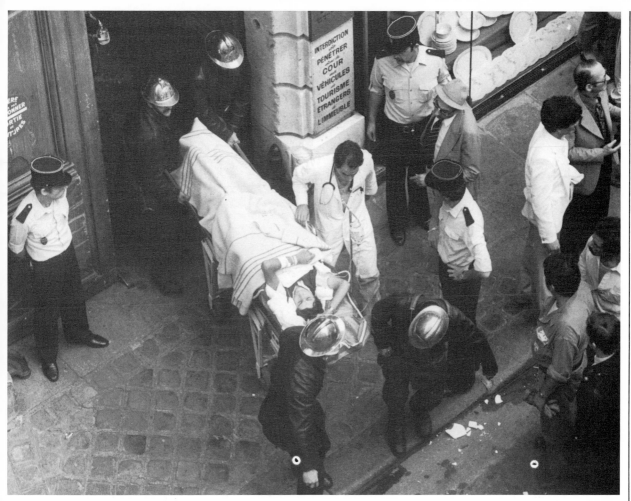

bombs are rendered harmless by robot or other controlled explosions. When this is impossible, it comes down to human skill and courage. Death is possible at any moment.

On the ward In any violent incident, it is often the doctors and nurses who show humanity in its best light. They treat all human beings impartially, terrorist and victim, soldier and rebel, regardless of background. Is it right for terrorists to receive treatment in this way when they have brought about their injuries by their own deeds? Are there ever occasions when the medical profession and the other emergency services should refuse to treat terrorists? Might this act as a deterrent?

Terrorists who are already prepared to take part in suicide attacks are unlikely to be deterred by such action. Doctors must honour the traditions of their profession and not take sides: all human life is of equal value. To act otherwise would in itself be a form of terrorism.

International help In many human or natural disasters, the International Red Cross, or its Islamic equivalent, the Red Crescent, often play an important part. Nevertheless, the 1977 Geneva Protocol under which the Red Cross operates, does not extend to the terrorists themselves.

'Mercy has a human heart.'
William Blake (1757-1827)

In major terrorist crisis areas, political tension can be defused by bringing in neutral United Nations troops to police the area. These soldiers are drawn from the armies of non-involved member nations. In recent years, United Nations troops have been active in Cyprus and Lebanon, running the risk of death or injury in the interests of international peace. The UNO is often criticized for being ineffective. Could such international peacekeeping forces not be deployed more often?

Six people were killed and 21 wounded when two terrorists opened fire with machine guns inside this restaurant. French police and doctors stand by as firemen carry a stretcher to the waiting ambulance.

Opposite Explosive detection experts wearing protective clothing search for ETA bombs in Malaga, Spain.

A world

Opposite A United Nations post in South Lebanon. Is international control and understanding the only lasting answer to terrorism?

On 25 June 1985, the United Kingdom finally reached agreement with the USA concerning extradition of Provisional IRA suspects. A previous American court ruling had upheld claims that such offences were 'political' and so not covered by existing procedures. Three days later, the member nations of the European Economic Community (EEC), meeting in Italy, launched a new anti-terrorist campaign.

The fight against terrorism had become a major international priority. The rapid escalation of terrorist incidents was proving a real threat to world stability. How would the problem be tackled?

International measures In the future, terrorism practised by individuals or groups, though not necessarily by governments, will be met with harsh counter-measures. These will include greater international cooperation, improved counter-intelligence, extensive legislation, harsher sentencing and increased security. New technology will be in the forefront of any campaign.

The most controversial area will be that of reprisals. 'Hawkish' politicians will argue for more military strikes, whether directed against specific or general targets, and demand secret assassination of opponents who use terrorist methods. The 'doves' will argue that such responses are inflammatory, illegal or immoral.

Room for hope Without any doubt, governments with a real desire to combat terrorism will have suitable weapons at their disposal. But will they succeed? Armour is never a substitute for understanding. The USA threw all its armed might into the Vietnam War during the 1960s and 70s, but it eventually lost because it failed to understand the motivation of the enemy. President Reagan was applauded by some for calling Colonel Qadhafi of Libya a 'mad dog' in April 1986, and for his subsequent bombing of Libya. But did he really understand Libya, or the Islamic world? Does the USSR understand why their convoys continue to be attacked in the mountain passes of Afghanistan?

All the world's major powers profess ideals, but practise expedience. Both eastern and western countries claim to be democratic in their own way, but are prepared to support repressive regimes and proponents of state terror, whilst manoeuvring for economic or political advantage. Is it small wonder that gaps appear in their credibility?

Any lasting solution to the growing problem of terrorism does not lie in more armoured cars or more propaganda, but in a breakdown of international hypocrisy, and a willingness to listen to the oppressed. The fact that, in December 1985, the UNO unanimously passed a motion condemning terrorism, might offer some hope for the future, if one did not have nagging doubts that the superpowers exercise expedience even as part of the peacemaking process. If

A sign of the times? British police, traditionally unarmed, carry machine guns at London's Heathrow Airport.

at peace?

an injustice is resolved, the motivation for terrorism goes with it. In seemingly intractable situations, surely governments should favour diplomacy to firepower? Reprisal may teach the terrorists a lesson, but is it the right one? Revenge breeds revenge.

If solution by political pressure and diplomacy seems an impossibly idealistic response, consider a world in which might is always right, in which terror by both state and individual goes unchecked. Could you live in it?

'. . . governments adhered to policy. Next time they should try thinking.'

Richard Cohen (on the Maltese hijack shootout) in the International Tribune, *November, 1985*

'The only way out of this is for us to start listening . . .'

Moorhead Kennedy, former US hostage in Iran

Reference

Organizations using armed violence

Action Directe – French leftist group, founded 1979. Links with W. German Red Army Faction.

African National Congress (ANC) – Originally a reformist movement, today a revolutionary organization combating state terror in S. Africa. Recognized by United Nations (UN) and Organization of African Unity (OAU). Members trained with Cuban advisors in Angola and Zaire.

Al Fatah (Movement of Palestinian National Liberation) – Set up in 1959 to promote armed struggle against Israeli state.

Angry Brigade – British anarchist group claiming responsibility for 1971 bombing campaign.

Black Panthers – US Black Power group advocating violence. Founded 1966 by Huey Newton and Bobby Seale.

Black September – Palestinian terrorist group responsible for murder of Israelis at the 1972 Olympic Games in Munich.

Breton Liberation Front (FLB) – Founded 1966, aiming to wrest Celtic Brittany from French control. One of several groups, some terrorist, some reformist or cultural.

Deutsche Aktionsgruppen (DA) – Neo-Nazi terrorists operating in Hamburg in 1981.

Egypt's Revolution – Libya-backed group responsible for 1985 Egyptair hijack.

Ethniki Organosis Kyprion Agoniston (EOKA) – Greek Cypriot organization leading mid-1950s campaign against British troops. Sought union with Greece.

Euskadi ta Askatasuna (ETA) – Active movement seeking Basque secession from Spain. Terrorist acts after devolution moves suspended by central government. Assassination of police and bombing campaign.

Free South Moluccan Youth (VZJ) – Train hijackers and terrorists from former Dutch colony, active in Netherlands in the 1970s.

Free Wales Army (FWA) – Organization carrying out bombing campaign in Wales in late 1960s. Failed to get widespread nationalist support.

Grey Wolves – Extreme right-wing organization terrorizing Turkish leftists in 1970s. Backed by state.

Hizbollah (Party of God) – Shiite Moslem organization active in Lebanon 1985.

Irgun Zvai Leumi (National Military Organization) – Jewish terrorist organization active in Palestine before 1948. Organizer, Menachem Begin, later Israeli premier.

Irish National Liberation Army (INLA) – Military wing of Irish Republican Socialist Party. Split from Official IRA in 1974. Terrorist attacks in N. Ireland and on British mainland.

Irish Republican Army – Official (IRA) – Founded 1919; predecessors included 19th century Fenian societies, and Irish Volunteers. Fought guerrilla war against British troops in Ireland and a terrorist campaign on the mainland. Aims for united Irish republic. Ceasefire declared in N. Ireland in 1972.

Irish Republican Army – Provisional (Prov. IRA) – Founded 1969 following split from Official IRA over their Marxist policy. Most active terrorist group in N. Ireland and British mainland, killing troops, police and civilians. Aims for united Irish republic.

LEHI ('Stern Gang') – Jewish terrorist organization active prior to creation of Israeli state in 1948.

Liberation Tigers – One of terrorist groups active in Sri Lanka, supporting Tamil minority against Sinhalese government.

Makaz-i-Milli (National Islamic Front for Afghanistan) – Founded in 1979; one of many guerrilla factions fighting Afghani government and Soviet troops of occupation.

Mau Mau – Kikuyu movement opposing British rule in Kenya. Active 1950s.

Mudiad Amddiffyn Cymru (MAC) – Welsh separatist organization engaged in bombing campaign, 1960s.

Montoneros – Argentinian Peronist group of 1970s, responsible for series of assassinations.

National Liberation Army (ELN) – Rural-based guerrilla movement fighting Bolivian government in 1960s. Veteran supporter Ernesto 'Che' Guevara d 1967.

National Liberation Front (FLN) – Founded 1954, Algerian organization fighting French colonists.

Organisation de l'Armée Secrète (OAS) – Terrorist organization of French colonists in Algeria prior to independence in 1962.

Palestinian Liberation Organization (PLO) – Coordinating organization for Palestinian liberation movements, some of which have used terrorist tactics. Founded in 1964.

People's Revolutionary Army (ERP) – Practised kidnap, bank robbery and assassination in Argentina in 1970s. Wing of Argentinian Workers' Revolutionary Party.

Polisario – Guerrillas disputing Moroccan control of former Spanish Sahara, active in 1980s.

Popular Front for the Liberation of Angola (MPLA) – Founded 1956. Guerrilla war against Portuguese colonists prior to 1975. Subsequent consolidation of power against rivals.

Popular Front for the Liberation of Palestine (PFLP – Jebha) – Leading proponent of terrorism in its fight against state of Israel.

Québec Liberation Front (FLQ) – French-Canadian separatist movement established 1963. Notorious for 1970 kidnap of British trade commissioner James Cross, and murder of politician Pierre Laporte.

Rebel Armed Forces (FAR) – One of many revolutionary groups operating in Guatemala, founded 1962.

Red Army Faction (RAF) – Groupings of leftist anarchists active in West Germany in the 1970s, including the Baader-Meinhof group. International terrorist campaign.

Red Army – Japan (Sekigun) – Japanese terrorist organization founded 1969, led by Tsuneo Mori. Cooperated with Palestinians in Israel, Singapore, Kuwait.

Red Brigades – Leftist terrorists active in Italy during 1970s and early 1980s.

Revolutionary Cells – W. German left-wing commandos active in 1970s and 80s.

South West African People's Organization (SWAPO) – Guerrillas fighting illegal occupation of Namibia by Republic of South Africa.

Symbionese Liberation Army (Taking its name from 'symbiosis', in the sense of co-operation) – US urban terrorists in 1970s, notorious for Patty Hearst kidnap saga.

Tartan Army – Name given to supporters of Scottish Republican Socialist League; 7 jailed in 1982 on charges of conspiracy and bank robbery.

Tigre People's Liberation Front – Ethiopian separatist movement of 1970s and 80s.

Tupamaros (MLN) – Urban guerrilla group active in Uruguay 1960s and 70s.

Ulster Defence Association (UDA) – N. Ireland 'loyalist' terror organization founded in 1971.

Ulster Volunteer Force (UVF) – Founded 1966, 'loyalist' opponents of IRA.

Glossary

Arson – The burning down of buildings.

Anarchism – A social theory opposing rule by government: instead, society should function by cooperation between groups or individuals. Some anarchists advocate violence, some reject it.

Blood feud – A tradition whereby a family or tribe seek revenge for death or injury to one of its members.

Capitalism – An economic and social system based on private ownership of the means of production.

Censorship – The suppression of material to be published, broadcast or otherwise communicated.

Civil disobedience – The refusal to obey laws or pay taxes on political grounds.

Colonialism – 1) A policy of one nation ruling another. 2) A national policy of foreign settlement.

Communism – 1) Belief in a social system based on common ownership. 2) Belief in a totalitarian social system in which the means of production are state-owned. 3) In Marxist theory, the end product of socialism.

Counter-revolutionary – Opposing revolutionary policies.

Crusade – 1) A religious war fought by Christians. 2) A campaign fought for any cause.

Dictator – A ruler who assumes absolute power.

Ethics – A system of morals.

Fascism – A totalitarian social system based on state authority and aggressive nationalism; anti-socialist.

Freedom fighter – Someone who engages in armed struggle to free a country from occupation or oppression.

Genocide – The mass murder of a race or nation.

Guerrilla – 1) *n.* An irregular soldier engaged in the harrassment of enemy troops. 2) *adj.* The kind of irregular warfare which avoids pitched battle.

Hijack – 1) To steal in transit. 2) To take over a plane or other means of transport and threaten the crew or passengers.

Hostage – A person forcibly held as a bargain to ensure security of captor or the fulfilment of captor's demands.

Hunger strike – Refusal to take food as a means of political protest.

Ideology – The theories or ideals constituting a political system.

Interrogation techniques – Methods of questioning detainees: often harsh, they are intended to force the captive to reveal information against his or her will.

Irredentism – The policy of incorporating certain territory within a state on the grounds of common culture or ethnic background.

Jihad – 1) A holy war fought by Moslems. 2) Any campaign for a cause.

Judiciary – The judges and court system.

'Just' war – Warfare which is believed to be justified on moral grounds because it opposes a greater evil.

Kidnap – To abduct someone in order to extort money or political concessions.

Legitimacy – Legal acceptability.

Martyrdom – This religious term is sometimes used to describe the process whereby a victim who dies for a cause receives widespread admiration.

Marxism – Belief in the political theories proposed by Karl Marx and his followers, which claimed that economic change is brought about by class struggle as part of an inevitable political process.

Morals – The principles by which one decides whether behaviour is right or wrong.

Mujihadeen – Islamic revolutionaries or irregulars.

Nationalism – 1) The pursuit of independence as a nation. 2) The pursuit of national interests above all others or policies of national self-aggrandizement.

Nazism – National Socialism; totalitarian political system developed in Germany under Adolf Hitler, based on aggression, racism and authoritarianism.

Neofascism or *Neonazism* – Nationalist and racist views similar to those of Mussolini or Hitler which have re-emerged in our own day.

Nihilism – 1) A disbelief in moral principles. 2) In Tsarist Russia, a belief that all existing social institutions had to be destroyed and then replaced.

Partisan – 1) *adj.* Supporting a particular cause or bias. 2) *n.* A guerrilla fighting for his or her country against an invading or occupying force.

Propaganda – Information or misinformation intended to convert people to a political or religious cause.

Racism or *racialism* – Theories or practices based on a belief in racial differentiation, often discriminatory and offensive to people of another race.

Reign of terror – 1) A period during the French Revolution when many opponents of the ruling group were executed. 2) Any similar period of state terror.

Resistance – A secret organization continuing to fight occupying enemy troops after their country has been defeated.

Sabotage – Disruption of work or supply by means of spoiling or destruction.

Sectarian – Having to do with a religious sect.

Socialism – 1) Belief in a social system based on public ownership of the means of production. 2) Belief in a degree of public ownership within a liberal capitalist democracy. 3) In Marxist theory, a stage on the road to Communism.

State terrorism – The use by a government of armed violence, torture or murder to overcome opposition to state policy.

Suicide attack – An act of violence in which both attacker and victim are intended to die.

Separatism – The policy of territorial secession from a nation state.

Totalitarian – Allowing no political opposition.

Further reading

A Dictionary of Modern Revolution by Edward Hyams (Allen Lane, 1973). Alphabetical listing related to terrorism, revolution, movements and individuals.

Northern Ireland: A Political Directory by W. D. Flackes (BBC, 1980). Alphabetical listing of politics, personalities, and history, with statistical charts.

The New State of the World Atlas (Pan, 1984). Maps which graphically catalogue the world's economic and political problems, crisis regions and terrorist states.

The World Atlas of Revolutions by Andrew Wheatcroft (Hamish Hamilton, 1983). Detailed maps accompanying informative text; case studies of terror campaigns, guerrilla warfare and revolution.

The Challenge of Youth (Revolutions of Our Time) by Friedrich Heer (Weidenfeld & Nicolson, 1974). Illustrated guide to the history of revolutionary and terrorist youth movements.

Children of War by Roger Rosenblatt (New English Library, 1983). The author meets children from the world's crisis areas, including Northern Ireland, Israel and Cambodia.

A Criminal History of Mankind by Colin Wilson (Granada, 1984). A depressing but readable book. Its scope takes in the Ismaili order of Assassins and the Baader-Meinhof group.

The Disappeared: Voices of a Secret War by John Simpson and Jana Bennett (Robson Books, 1985). Moving account of the victims of state terror and death squads in Argentina.

The Disarmer's Handbook by Andrew Wilson (Penguin, 1983). Guide to international security, intelligence gathering, the ethics of warfare and nuclear weapons. Suitable for peace studies.

The War of the Flea by Robert Taber (Paladin, 1969). Studies on guerrilla warfare. Includes observations on early IRA tactics, EOKA, and campaigns in North Africa and Malaysia in the 1950s.

Anarchism by George Woodcock (Pelican, 1963). A classic account of anarchist theory, non-violent and violent, and the tactics it has inspired.

Political Killings by Governments by Amnesty International, 1983. Documents state assassination in 20 countries.

Torture in the Eighties by Amnesty International, 1984. Documents the extent to which state torture is used as a tactic of state terror in the modern world.

Educational films

The Bounds of Freedom – No. 6: Terrorism: Video cassette, colour, 52 minutes
Hire or sale from Concord Films Council. Examines the role of the media in relation to terrorism. From Granada's State of the Nation series.

One Word of Truth: 16mm film, colour, 29 minutes
Hire from Educational Foundation for Visual Aids. Soviet dissident Alexander Solzhenitsyn's account of prison camps is taken as the basis of a wide-ranging look at issues such as violence and terrorism, the state and the individual, and the role of the artist.

When the Mountain Trembles: 16mm film or video cassette, b/w, 83 minutes
Hire from Concord Films Council. Account of state terrorism in Guatemala 1954–83, narrated by a Quichi Indian.

Useful addresses

International Institute for Strategic Studies, 23 Tavistock Street, London WC2

Concord Films Council, 201 Felixstowe Road, Ipswich, Suffolk IP3 9BJ, England

Educational Foundation for Visual Aids, George Building, Coleg Normal, Bangor, Gwynedd LL57 2PZ, Wales

Index

The numbers in **bold** refer to illustrations and captions.

Credits

The author and publishers
would like to thank the
following for their kind
permission to reproduce
copyright illustrations:

Aldus Archive: 8
Associated Press: 37
Camera Press: 22, 26–7, 44
Popperfoto: 7, 11, 23, 29, 34, 38,
    41, 42, 47, 48–9
Rex: cover, 4, 12–13, 21
    (bottom), 25, 30, 31, 35, 56
Rex/SIPA: 5, 6, 9, 10, 14, 16, 17,
    18–19, 21 (top), 27 (top), 28,
    33 (both), 36, 39, 40, 43, 45,
    46, 49 (top), 50, 51, 53, 54,
    55, 57